Conte[nts]

Acknowledgements.

The Six Dales Trail project was devised and developed by a small team from Otley 'Walkers Are Welcome'. (See page 42) The group included members of the Ramblers' Association, Otley Walkers, and the Long Distance Walkers Association. One of the team, John Sparshatt, pioneered both the route and this guide to it. The project was generously funded by the Nidderdale Area of Outstanding Natural Beauty, and was supported throughout by its officers. The Long Distance Walkers Association made a financial contribution towards the cost of the project. The Transport Projects Officer of Leeds Metro advised on the public transport and tourism aspects of the project. The Rights of Way team at North Yorkshire County Council supplied both expertise and practical support in the form of waymarking and footbridge repairs. Otley Town Council's Community Development Officer contributed help and advice. The photographs in this guide were taken by members of Otley Camera Club, by members of the working group, or were supplied by officers of the Nidderdale Area of Outstanding Natural Beauty.
Dolf Middelhoff designed the Six Dales Trail logo.

* Jan Bartholomew, Michael Bartholomew, Peter Corkill, Stuart Fildes, Jur Keessen, Gerald McGowan, Randal Metzger, John Morgan, John Sparshatt

About the author.

John Sparshatt has been a keen walker for over 30 years. He is a long-standing member and officer of the Long Distance Walkers Association (LDWA) and a member of the West Yorkshire group of the LDWA. He has organised three of the LDWA flagship 100-mile challenge events and two annual local challenge events over the past 30 years. He is co-editor of the 2009 UK Trailwalkers Handbook a comprehensive directory of over 1400 long distance paths and has revised the popular Centenary Way, from York to Filey, walk guide. He is co-authoring the Welcome Way, a 28-mile circular route linking the Walkers are Welcome Communities of Otley, Burley in Wharfedale and Baildon.

First published by Walkers are Welcome (Otley) 2010 www.waw-otley.org.uk
Second edition, revised 2011
Third Edition revised 2016
Copyright © Walkers are Welcome - Otley
Maps printed under licence from Ordnance Survey
OS Licence 100047385
ISBN 978-0-9564441-1-0
Photo of Janet Street-Porter by Randal Metzger.
Designed and Printed by Bowland Graphics

Foreword
by Janet Street-Porter

 ve lived in Upper Nidderdale for over thirty years, and spent hours exploring arts of this route in all weathers and all seasons.....Being an avid map-reader I worked out how to walk from south to north following paths and old bridleways, and then all I needed at the end of the day was a lift back home. This trail links the places where all you will hear is the sound of grouse and a stiff breeze. You'll pick bilberries and see brown trout. But most of all you'll find solitude. What could be more enjoyable than standing on the moortop and looking down into Coverdale, with its patchwork of green fields and dry stone walls? North Yorkshire is full of hidden delights and this guide should encourage you to be adventurous and enjoy more than one dale in a day!

anet Street-Porter

ormer President Ramblers' Association.

Otley from the Chevin

Introduction

The Six Dales Trail, in North Yorkshire, runs for 38 miles (61kms) through the Nidderdale Area of Outstanding Natural Beauty, from Otley, in Wharfedale, northwards to Middleham, in Wensleydale. Along its way it crosses the 5 watersheds that separate the six dales and that give the trail its name. From Wharfedale it passes over into Washburndale, then into Nidderdale, Colsterdale, Coverdale and finally Wensleydale. The trail runs the length of the Nidderdale Area of Outstanding Natural Beauty, traversing some of the finest dales landscapes in Yorkshire.

There is not a dull patch on the trail. It starts from the ancient market town of Otley on the River Wharfe. It makes its way northwards, often along little-used field paths threading across sheep pastures bordered by ancient stone walls, into Washburndale, a dale whose river has been dammed in order to create three reservoirs, alongside which the trail passes. The trail then climbs over a watershed and heads down through woodland to Glasshouses, on the River Nidd. The Nidd is followed, upstream, to Pateley Bridge, a small market town in the heart of Nidderdale. From there, the trail first stays close to the Nidd and then runs alongside one of the dale's reservoirs, Gouthwaite. From the northern end of the reservoir, the trail climbs out of Nidderdale up onto vast Fountains Earth moor, before dropping down into little-known Colsterdale and the hamlet of Gollinglith. Another climb takes the trail over superb moorland to a watershed which opens up a view of lower Wensleydale. The trail descends from the moors down to Ellingstring, and then across pastures to the grand, wooded, eighteenth-century parkland surrounding the ruins of twelfth century Jervaulx Abbey. From the Abbey the trail joins the bank of the river Ure, Wensleydale's chief river. A few miles upstream the Ure is joined by one of its tributaries, the Cover. The trail follows the bank of the Cover,

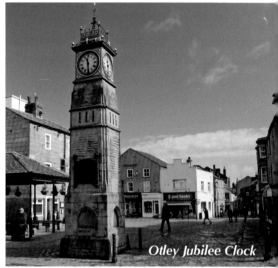

Otley Jubilee Clock

through well-wooded country, for a few miles before making its final, decisive turn up the hillside and over the brow to reveal the dramatic sight of Middleham Castle and, beyond it, the little town of Middleham.

Along the trail, walkers can expect to see plenty of birds, among them curlews, lapwings, buzzards, red kites (which have flourished since their recent re-introduction), red grouse, skylarks, golden plovers and dippers bobbing on rocks in the rivers. The moorlands are transformed in late summer by the extraordinary blaze of colour of the heather, but there is plenty of interest at other seasons. Cotton-grass, bilberry, mosses and lichens border the trail. The rock that underlies the trail is mainly gritstone, which outcrops in substantial, handsome crags in many places. It also supplies the stone for the miles and miles of dry stone walls, for the fabric of the farms and the

Otley's medieval bridge over the River Wharfe

buildings of the towns and villages through which the trail passes. One of the many attractions of the trail is its sequence of old stone stiles: some are gap stiles – known locally as 'squeeze bellies' (just wide enough for a walker, but too narrow for a sheep) – and some are step stiles, built to get walkers over walls that can be over 5 feet high.

Accommodation for walkers is abundant in some places, but scarce in others. There are only a few campsites. The Six Dales Trail website (www.sixdalestrail.org.uk) contains a regularly-updated list of accommodation on, or close to, the trail. It is not exhaustive, though. Enquiries at the local tourist information centres in Otley, Pateley Bridge and Leyburn may result in further possibilities (See pages 38-41). The website also provides information about organised walks along the trail and about baggage transfers between accommodation addresses.

The trail is well-served by public transport. Accurate details of services cannot be printed in this guide, for timetables change from year to year; but the main outlines are clear. Otley is well-supplied with buses from major urban centres such as Leeds and Bradford (including Leeds-Bradford airport), and can be reached by train and shuttle bus from nearby Menston station, which in turn links into the main rail network via Leeds and Bradford. Buses can be picked up at Pateley Bridge and Middleham, and a return to Otley, via Ripon and Harrogate should be possible. More details of the buses serving various places on the trail are set out later in this guide, in the sections on Otley, Pateley Bridge and Middleham.

The Six Dales Trail website will attempt to keep up with changes in public transport provision, and this guide gives the phone numbers and websites of tourist information centres and bus operators.

The trail has no major physical hazards: it goes over no high mountains, and it does not go close to dangerous, sheer edges. But it does traverse some

Above Bouthwaite towards Gouthwaite Reservoir

remote moorland, and it is sometimes rough and wet underfoot. Only the super-fit will attempt the 38-mile trail in one go: most people will want a more leisurely pace and will break the route down into shorter stages.
As in all remote locations in wild country, sudden changes in conditions - snow, or rises in river levels for example - can cause trouble. The walker therefore needs to be equipped with all-weather gear, and decent footwear, whatever the season. The trail is waymarked with fingerposts and roundels in both directions bearing the Six Dales Trail logo. These waymarks will help to keep the walker on track, but they will not be sufficient in themselves. Careful use of both the route descriptions and the maps on the following pages will be necessary.

A compass will be extremely useful, not just for orienting the walker in poor visibility on high moorland stretches of the trail but, equally, to keep her or him heading in the right direction when the trail winds through woods or across fields.

KEY

Each of the 14 stages of the trail is set out across two facing pages of this guide. On the left hand page, there is a numbered prose description of the stage. On the facing, right hand, page there is a map of the stage, based on the 1:25000 Ordnance Survey map. The scale of the maps varies somewhat from page to page, but in every map the blue coloured squares are 1km along each side. On the maps the route is indicated by a corridor bordered in purple. The corridor is wide enough for the underlying detail to be seen. The walker needs to be able to discover, from the map, whether she or he is following a footpath, a bridleway, or a tarmac road, or where the walls run. The prose description is numbered, and the maps are keyed with the corresponding numbers, so that the user can speedily relate description and map. The prose description of the route is in black. Points of particular interest along the route, or close to it, are in blue, and are numbered in blue on the maps. On the ground, the trail is waymarked by signs and plaques bearing the Six Dales Trail Logo. This guide is designed to equip walkers with all they need in the way of maps. But for those who like to have the complete OS sheets in their hands, four from the Explorer series, numbers 297, 298, 302, and OL30 will be needed. The route is fully marked on the OS mapping with green diamonds.

Track up from Gouthwaite Dam

Regular updates about the trail, and information about accommodation and public transport can be found on the Six Dales Trail website: www.sixdalestrail.org.uk

Clear & Sunny 6mL.
13/4/19

1. Otley to Clifton (2.3 miles)

1. The trail starts at the Jubilee Clock in Market Place, next to the Butter Cross. Walk to the traffic lights and cross Market Place into the right hand side of Manor Square.

2. The historic Market Town of Otley, with shops and accommodation is the birthplace of 17th Century cabinet-maker and furniture designer Thomas Chippendale. There are bus links to Menston train station, Ilkley, Leeds, Bradford, Harrogate and Skipton. See page 38.

3. Continue to the far end of Manor Square and then turn right. A statue of Thomas Chippendale stands on the opposite side of the road (Clapgate) outside the ancient grammar school. Go to the end of Clapgate and turn left into Bridge Street. Follow it down to the bridge over the River Wharfe.

4. Cross the bridge and, 20 yards before the light-controlled crossing, take the footpath on the left. The path quickly reaches Kell Beck, which flows alongside the right hand side. Follow the path ahead over the grassed area and then on a good surfaced path which becomes a lane and reaches a road (Weston Road).

5. Cross Weston Road, go left, and then immediately right into Weston Drive. The beck is still on your right and the path ahead is over the grassed area. Follow the beck to a road bridge (Weston Ridge) over the beck.

6. Cross the bridge and enter the enclosed footpath opposite, now with the beck on your left and Otley Hospital grounds to the right. Continue up this path, reaching another road (St Richard's Road). Cross this and continue ahead up the enclosed path to reach another road (St David's Road).

7. Turn right on St David's Road and after 300 yards turn left at a footpath sign (Clifton/Weston) on the left. Follow the path between the houses to a kissing gate into a field. Go through the gate and follow the path half-left and up the hill. At the top of the rise, cross the field to a bridle gate in the far left corner.

8. Go through the gate and turn left with the hedge on the left. Follow this path to a gate. Go through the gate and ahead to cross a stream at the side of a large tree, then half right across the field, turning left past a field corner and then ahead to a small metal gate.

9. Go through the gate and then ahead towards a wood (East Wood) and a track. Turn sharp right on the track just before the wood and ascend to a gate. Go through the gate and continue on the track to reach a bridle gate, then through this gate into an enclosed sunken lane. Follow the lane up the hill to reach a farm track and then a tarmac road leading into Clifton hamlet. (Note the many attractive buildings in this settlement.)

10. Follow the road through Clifton to reach the main road (Newall Carr Road). Cross over with care and climb over the stile opposite (signed 'Farnley') into the field. Cross the field in an easterly direction, with Otley Communication mast on your left, to a gate hidden from view down by a stream.

Clifton

11

Haddockstones
Plantation

207

Haddockstones
Farm

10

Yew Tree
Farm

Carr Side

48

New Gate rear of St Davids Rd

NEWALL WI
CLIFTON O

FA

Ne

Peashills
Plantation

8

Carr Banks
Gill

Copmanroyd
Farm

9

47

7

Carr
Bank

School

W

Newall

Hospl

6

Schs

5

Sch

FB

Weir

Mill

46

Pipe Lin

e Nest
m

Ashfield
House

Six Dales
Trail

Otley
Bridge

4

52

2

Coll

Sand and Gravel
Pits

3

Sch

Ordnance
Survey®

Licence No. 100047385
Grid Lines = 1kilometre
Kilometre=0.6214 Miles
Mile=1.6093 Kilometres

2. Clifton to Timble Gill Beck (4 miles)

11. Drop down to the gate go through it, cross the stream, and then cross over a stile in a wall on the right. Turn left and, still heading east, follow the path for 400 yards, with initially a wall then a fence on your left, to a small gate on the left.

12. Go through this gate and follow the wall on the right for 100 yards to a stone stile. Go over the stile and head northwards, diverging steadily from the wall until you see a conifer plantation ahead. Head towards the right-hand corner of the plantation where you will find a gate next to a very small marked reservoir. Go through the gate and head downhill with a wall and Crag Plantation on your left to reach a gate and track opposite Crag Farm.

13. Go through the gate and turn left on the track. Follow the track, passing through another gate, for 0.8 of a mile, following the track as it swings leftwards, (SE 199493) and through another gate, up an enclosed lane, to reach the tarmac road near Bride Cross House.

14. Turn right and follow the road, passing Bride Cross House on your right, and Middle Farm on your left. The road eventually becomes a track. Follow the track down to Dob Park Packhorse Bridge, which spans the River Washburn.

15. Turn left just before the bridge through the metal gate and, with the River Washburn on your right, follow the footpath northwards, upstream, through gates and stiles, through a wood, crossing two streams, always with the river on your right, to reach Timble Gill Beck at SE 188517 after 0.9 miles.
(Note: formerly, the beck was crossed here by a famous little arched stone footbridge, dedicated to the memory of Arthur Adamson, a stalwart member of the Ramblers' Association. Sadly, the bridge was washed away in a flood in July 2009.)

Dob Park packhorse bridge

11 May wet, Sunny (2 +3) 8mle

3. Timble Gill Beck to Blubberhouses (3.6 miles)

16. Cross Timble Gill Beck and turn left for 50 yards to reach a wall corner. Turn right up the hill, initially keeping the wall on your left. After 200 yards, strike half-right across the field to reach the far top right hand corner. Go through the gateway on the right, turn left, and now with the wall on the left, follow the path to another gate.

17. Go through this gate into an enclosed lane. Follow this lane to reach Nether Timble Farm. The track (High Lane) runs between the farm buildings. Pass through two gates at the farm and a further three gates on the track ahead. Continue on High Lane to reach a gate and stile (Swinsty Reservoir sign) on the right, 0.4 mile from Nether Timble Farm.

18. Turn right over the stile and descend through the wood for 200 yards to reach a permissive path on the left just before the buildings at Swinsty Hall. Turn left and follow this path to join another track. Turn left, and follow this track for 0.6 mile to the car park at Swinsty Moor.

19. Public lavatories. At weekends and summer months, there is often an ice cream van and sometimes other refreshment vehicles.

20. Leave the car park and cross the road to the footpath opposite. Take this path down to Fewston reservoir and the reservoir edge path. Follow this reservoir path (reservoir on right) for 1.9 miles to the car park at Blubberhouses. (*According to the Penguin dictionary of English place names, the name 'Blubberhouses' comes from the Old and Middle English for 'houses by the bubbling stream'.*)

21. Accommodation (B & B) nearby at Scaife Hall. There is a very limited bus service, the X75, which runs on Saturdays only, operated by York Pullman (01904 622992). The nearest bus stop is 400 yards to the right on the main road, outside the pub, but buses will stop anywhere safe, if they are hailed.

Swinsty

4. Blubberhouses to Water Tower on Greenhow Hill Road (2.8 miles)

22. Cross the road from the car park at Blubberhouses and descend the steps to the eastern bank of the River Washburn. Follow the riverside path upstream for 1.7 miles, in a north-westerly direction, with the river on your left. (As you walk up the path, notice the old goit, or millrace, that used to feed the water-powered flax mill – now long gone - at Blubberhouses. The goit runs parallel to the trail, on the right.) Just after you pass a tall fir tree on your left, at about 300 yards below the dam of Thruscross Reservoir, turn left from the track and cross the footbridge over the river. At the end of the bridge, take the path, uphill for 100 yards. At a junction with a track, turn left and then immediately right, up a short bank to meet a tarmac dam service road. Turn right and walk for 400 yards down towards the left hand end of the dam. Just before a gate at the terminus of the tarmac, take the stepped path, on the left hand side, that ascends through woodland for 200 yards to join the road that passes across the dam.

23. Thruscross Reservoir was completed in 1966, much later than the other three reservoirs in Washburndale, which are nineteenth century. The construction of the reservoir flooded the village of West End, which was already largely derelict following the decline of the flax industry. The remains of the flax mill can be seen at the edge of the reservoir and more of the village is revealed in times of drought. The reservoir is central to the plot of Peter Robinson's 'Inspector Banks' crime novel, *In a dry season*.

24. Cross the Dam and follow the road around to the left and then, just past the house on the right, join a path on the left that runs parallel to the road, just inside the wood. After 0.3 miles, at the point where the path turns downhill to the left towards the reservoir, leave the path and re-join the road to your right.

25. On the road, turn left up the hill and pass several houses on the left called Ratten Row. Near the top of the hill join a path on the left signed Greenhow Hill Road. Head northwards across this large field, initially with a wall on your left, and then head towards a water tower. Cross a stile onto the road.

Thruscross Reservoir

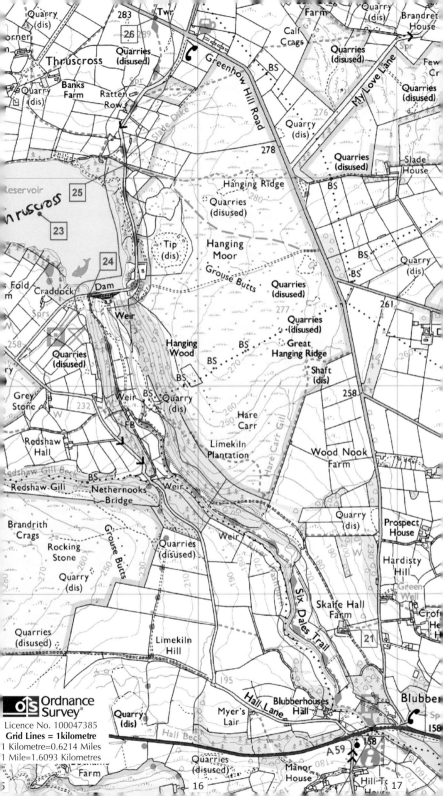

5. Water Tower on Greenhow Hill Road to Hall Field House Farm (1.2 miles)

26. Cross the road with care, through a gate into the field opposite. Follow the field edge down the hill, with a wall on your right, over two fields and then into a narrow field. Join a hard track, heading still in the same direction, through a metal gate and down through a farm yard, then through a gate, to reach the road at Padside Green.

27. Cross the road and over the stone stile on the opposite side of the road. Go through some rubble and with buildings on the left keep heading north to descend the field and reach a footbridge over a stream. Cross the bridge and follow the path to a stone stile.

28. Go over the stile and up the hill with the wall on the right, over a stone stile and through 2 gates, passing the ruins of Bents House on your left, to reach a track. Cross the track into the field beyond, and, heading in a northerly direction, cross this field to a stone stile in the far wall.

29. Cross this stile and go northwards to reach a stile near a fingerpost. Cross this stile and then across the track to a stone stile. Go over this stile into a field and aim for the three garage doors in one of the buildings in Hall Field House farm. Cross the stile in the fence onto the track in front of the farm.

30. Turn right onto the track for twenty yards and then left, passing between the farmhouse and the big barn. Pass through the farm yard, through a gate and cross a stream via the farm track, to reach a field gate. Go through the gate and, now with a wall on the left, follow the field edge, in a north-easterly direction, over 2 stone stiles, until you reach the large modern farm buildings of Woodman Wray Farm on your left. Keeping the buildings, and the wall you have been following, still on your left, go through a gate and on to a stone stile in the corner of the field.

Stile near Hall Field House Farm

6. Hall Field House Farm to High Hood Gap (2 miles)

31. Cross this stile in the corner of the field, then cross a small stream, turn right and follow the wall, on the left, to a gate. Grange Farm is now ahead of you. Cross 2 further stiles and pass an old chapel now converted to a dwelling, keeping this on your left. Follow the farm track, passing Grange House on your right, to reach the road at Dyke Lane Head farm. The right of way goes between the buildings (empty in 2016) via 2 stone stiles, but the more convenient farm track passing to the right of the buildings may be preferred. Either way, emerge on to the tarmac of Dyke Lane.

32. Turn left and northwards on the road. Follow it for 400 yards. Just past the right turn to Heyshaw, cross the stile on the right into the field. Cross the field diagonally, uphill, in a northerly direction, to a stile in the far wall. Cross this stile and head across the field, in the same direction, to another stile.

33. Cross the stile and head towards the buildings ahead at Hill Top, with the view down into Nidderdale opening up ahead. Join the track at Hill Top and, now on the Nidderdale Way, turn left and continue north, through the gate, for 800 yards.

34. 100 yards before the house at High Hood Gap (SE 171629) go through the gate in the wall on the right. Cross the field half-left in a northerly direction, going through a gap in the wall ahead, to follow the path, passing a wall corner. Keeping the wall on your left, walk to a stile in the wall.

Across Nidderdale from Hill Top

7. High Hood Gap to Pateley Bridge (2.1 miles)

35. Cross over the stile on to rough ground and a path. Head downhill, turning left across the slope (northwards) and into Guisecliff Wood.

36. Follow the clear track/path through the wood beneath Guisecliff for 600 yards. When the main path turns right, follow it downhill.

37. Guisecliff Tarn. This lake, which is well-worth seeing, is a few yards from the turn, close to a huge boulder on the left.

38. Continue winding steeply downhill in a northerly direction through Parker Wood to reach a stile. Exit the wood into an enclosed path. Continue downhill, passing Hollin Farm to your left, to reach Glasshouses Bridge over the River Nidd.

39. Cross the bridge and turn left into an enclosed track, with a small lake (an old mill dam) on your left. Follow this path, which soon joins the riverside path into Pateley Bridge.

Guise Cliff Tarn

8. Pateley Bridge to Coville Barn (3.6 miles)

40. Pateley Bridge, a Walkers are Welcome town. Shops, accommodation, lavatories, museum, buses to Harrogate and Ripon.
See notes about bus services on page 39.

41. Cross the main road in Pateley Bridge into the enclosed path near the main river bridge, and head north-west until you reach, after 300 yards, the riverside path.

42. Follow the riverside path, with the river on your left, for 1.6 miles, to Wath. Pass over the road at Wath, and continue on the riverside path to the stile at the bottom of Gouthwaite Reservoir. Cross the stile and head up the bank to join the track that runs along the eastern side of the Reservoir.

43. Turn left and follow this track, now signed 'Nidderdale Way' passing through several large gates, with the Reservoir on the left, for 1.4 miles to reach Coville Barn.

Gouthwaite Reservoir Dam

9. Coville Barn to Lulbeck Head (3.5miles)

44. There is B & B accommodation at Coville Barn, useful for doing the walk in three stages. There is also a pub in Ramsgill, just to the west of Bouthwaite This is the last place for refreshment and accommodation for the next 10 miles. See the website for more accommodation options.

45.   Continuing past Coville Barn on the good surfaced track for 0.7 miles to Bouthwaite, the trail now leaves the Nidderdale Way. Turn sharp right up the track at the junction and follow this track uphill for 0.9 miles to a track junction (SE 135718). There are good views back to Gouthwaite Reservoir as you climb the hill.

Note: the trail now enters open access land. The moorland may be closed from time to time, but the closures do not affect the public rights of way. The route of the trail is legally open at all times.

46. At the track junction turn left and follow this track northwards for 1.9 miles. Ignore the walled track branching off to the left after 0.5 miles and then reach a track junction (SE 140747). From this point, if the weather is clear, a view to the north-east, across the Vale of York to the Hambleton Hills, opens up. The White Horse at Kilburn should be visible (ENE).

Gouthwaite Reservoir from track above Bouthwaite

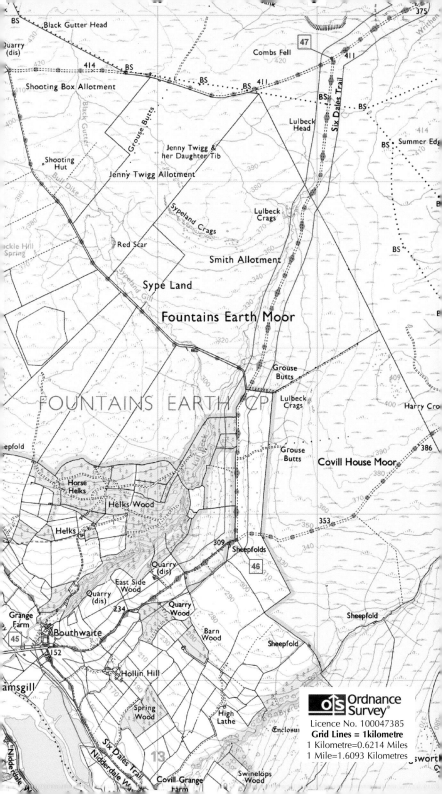

BS
Black Gutter Head
375
Quarry
(dis)
430
420
414 BS
Shooting Box Allotment
Combs Fell
47
411
420
BS
BS 411
Six Dales Trail
Summer Edge
400
Black Gutter
Bull Dike
Shooting Hut
Grouse Butts
Jenny Twigg &
her Daughter Tib
Jenny Twigg Allotment
Lulbeck
Head
BS
414
410
390
390
380
Red Scar
Speeland Gill
ckle Hill
Spring
Sypeland Crags
Lulbeck
Crags
Smith Allotment
370
350
BS
Sype Land
340
Fountains Earth Moor
330
320
FOUNTAINS EARTH CP
300
Grouse
Butts
Lulbeck
Crags
409
Harry Cro
400
386
epfold
Grouse
Butts
Covill House Moor
390
380
Horse
Helks
370
Helks Wood
Lulbeck
353
350
Helks
309
Sheepfolds
340
46
Quarry
(dis)
East Side
Wood
234
Quarry
(dis)
Quarry
Wood
290
Barn
Wood
Sheepfold
Sheepfold
Grange
Farm
45
Bouthwaite
210
152
Hollin Hill
amsgill
Spring
Wood
170
High
Lathe
Enclosur

os Ordnance
Survey
Licence No. 100047385
Grid Lines = 1kilometre
1 Kilometre=0.6214 Miles
1 Mile=1.6093 Kilometres

Six Dales Trail
Nidderdale Wa
13
Covill Grange
Farm
Swinelops
Wood
sworth

24/5/19

10. Lulbeck Head to Pott Moor High Road   (2.5 miles)

47. Turn right at this junction for 700 yards to find another track junction (SE 146750). Turn left here, through a metal barrier, and follow the track in a north-westerly direction to reach the shooting houses at Low Ash Head Moor.

Note: the next sections of the route require some careful navigation. Be sure to look ahead to the features specified in the following text, and keep a compass handy.

48. Cross the front of the shooting house and bear half-left for 10 yards to a large, wedge-shaped boulder. A heather moor descends ahead of you. On the far side of the valley beyond, a large farm, with modern barns – West Summer Side - is visible in clear weather. Leaving the wedge-shaped boulder on your right hand side, head down, half-right, across the heather moor in a northerly direction, keeping West Summer Side farm half-left ahead of you as a guide. After about 300 yards the little valley of Agill Beck comes into view. The beck feeds the 3 reservoirs – Agill Dam, Roundhill, and Leighton, which come into view half-right. Continue down the heather moor following the path and the cut through the heather, heading for Low Ash Head, the right-hand of the two derelict farms, to reach a field gate.

49. Go through the gate, then turn half-left to a gate in the wall that surrounds Low Ash Head. Pass through the gate, and then swing left around the left of the derelict main building, with old sheds on your left. Once through the farm buildings, head downhill, slightly right, to a stile half-way along the wall that faces you.

50. Cross over the stile, then half-right, making for a curved wall corner. Keeping this wall on your right, and Agill Beck below you on your left, walk on for 100 yards to meet a track. Turn left onto it and follow it as it curves to the right, through a gate, then trees and over 2 culverts supplying the reservoirs.

51. Emerging from the trees, walk uphill to the right, following a track across a field to find a small footbridge across a stream and a stile in the wall on the right.

52. Cross the stile. Look half-left and pick out your next destination, due north – a rusty-roofed shed on the horizon, by an electricity pole. Cross the large field ahead of you passing a yellow-topped marker post. Look out for a fallen, dead tree. It is just on the far side of a wall, near a wall junction, at the point where you'll find another footbridge and the next stile.

53. Cross this stile and, still heading north, cross the next field and go through a gate in its far top corner. Turn half-right and, heading uphill, reach a collection of derelict buildings (Summer Side). Keep the buildings on your left. After passing the final building – the rusty-roofed shed that you spied from point 52 - turn left for a few yards, and pass through a metal gate.

54.   Turn right and follow the field edge, with the wall on your right, for 200 yards, to a gate at Moorhead cottages. After 30 yards strike half-left across the big field with electricity poles in it to a stile. Go over the stile in the next wall then head north to another stile. Go over this one onto Pott Moor High Road, and turn right for 75 yards to a track on the left signed Grimes Gill House.

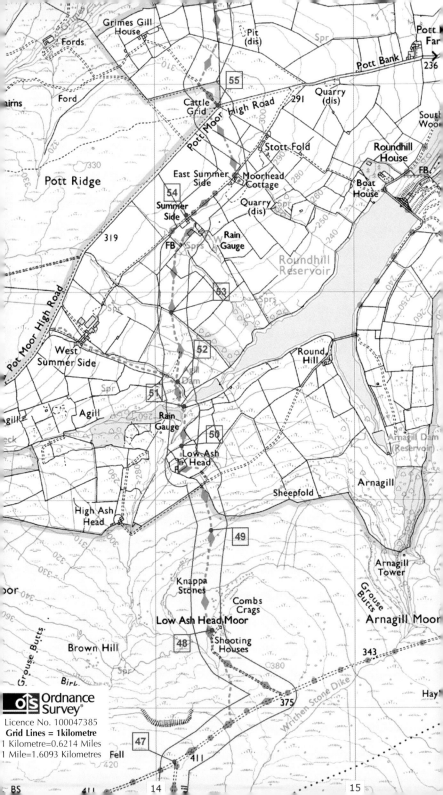

11. Pott Moor High Road to Leeds Pals Memorial (1.6 miles)

55. Take the track towards Grimes Gill House for 150 yards, as far as a cattle grid. Just across the grid, turn half-right and cross the field to a gate in the far corner. Go through the gate, and, with a wall on your left, go downhill to a further gate. Continue downhill through a small field to a metal gate. Go through the metal gate into a plantation.

56. Go downhill through the plantation, bearing steadily half-right and eventually crossing a small stream. Then pass through a gap near a wall corner and go downhill to find a footbridge crossing Grimes Gill (SE 143787). The footbridge is not marked on the OS map.

57. Cross the bridge and go uphill to a track. Cross this track to a broken stile (2016) in the plantation fence. Cross this stile and go uphill, through trees, to a double stile. Cross these into a field.

58. Continue uphill, with a wall on your right, to reach a track which leads between the buildings of derelict High Sourmire Farm. Cross the track, keeping all the farm buildings to your right, and, after 20 yards, cross a stile on your right, into a field. Cross this field half-left to a further stile. Cross this stile and traverse the field in a northerly direction, passing through the remains of an old field boundary (an ancient hedge), to find another stile in a wall.

59. Go over the stile, cross to the wall on the right, and follow it as far as a ladder stile next to a gate. Go over this stile and across the field to pass through a gate to the left of the buildings at Towler Hill onto a farm track.

60. Follow the farm track to the tarmac road. Turn right on the road for 450 yards, and go through a gate across the road.

61. A short diversion from the trail will take you to Leeds Pals Memorial, which is just 500 yards down the road. 'Pals' were army units composed of volunteers for service in the Great War of 1914-1918 who all came from one town, and who were therefore likely to have known each other, or at least to have had much in common. The Leeds Pals were brought to this remote spot, 35 miles from their homes in an industrial city, for training. Behind the memorial, you can see the remains of the foundations of the camp huts. Return now to the gate across the road to pick up the trail again.

Leeds Pals Memorial

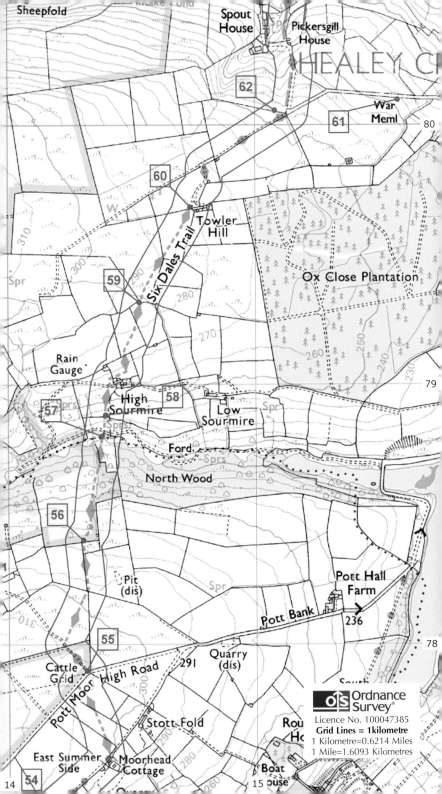

12. Leeds Pals Memorial to Ellingstring (2.8 miles)

62. If you are returning from the monument, just before you reach the gate across the road, turn right down a tarmac track. If you are not aiming to visit the monument, the tarmac track is on your left, just after the gate across the road. The tarmac track leads down to derelict Pickersgill House. Just before the ruin, leave the tarmac through a gate to the right of the building. Pass around behind the building to find a gate in a wall. Go through the gate, turn right, and descend the field to a bridle gate in the far corner. Go through the gate and across a bridge that spans a reservoir collection channel.

63. Continue onward, downhill, with a stream on your left, passing, on your right, a solitary, handsome old stone gate post. Turn half-right, diverging from the stream, and head for a large ash tree. Then, bear right, with a fence on your left, to find a bridle gate.

64. Go through the bridle gate and across the stream ahead. Go up the far bank and into a field. Cross this field half-right, keeping small barns to your left, to a gap in the hedge 100 yards from the barns. Go through this gap and cross the next field to the far side. Follow the path down a bank to a metal field gate. Go through this gate and turn right to the footbridge over the River Burn. Cross it, turn right on the tarmac road and immediately left up the track towards Agra Crags.

65. Follow the track uphill towards Low Agra Farm and, 100 yards before the farm, take the enclosed footpath through a small metal gate on the right. Continue uphill, ignoring the track to the left, and go through a gate, near a telegraph pole, into a field. Cross the field, half-left, to converge with the wall on your left. Follow the wall, to reach a gate in the far left corner of the field. The gate leads on to an enclosed track. Go through the gate onto the track, which runs along the left of the plantation at High Agra.

66. Just before the end of the enclosed track, take the gate on the left into a field. Go half-right across the field to a gate in the right hand wall. (The definitive footpath has been informally diverted here.)

67. Go through the gate and follow the farm track across two fields. The track is stoned in places, grassy in others. When you enter the second field you will see the track you need, 200 yards ahead of you, half-left, climbing a bank. At the third field, go through the gate. Ignore the stoned track to the right. Keep ahead on the faint grass track, with a wall on your left, across the field to a gate. (Small pond on right, near the gate.)

68. Go through the gate, ignoring the track that goes to the right, then ahead across boggy ground, to join the wall. Walk alongside this wall, keeping it to your left. Watch out for a fine old boundary stone inscribed 'Mashamshire' set in the wall. Ignore the ladder stiles that cross it and continue to a small gate through the wall near the plantation ahead (SE 163830). Go through the gate, turn right and follow the wall for 700 yards, (wall and plantation on right), as far as a gap in the wall, near a dead tree. The trail diverges here, and heads half-left, through the bilberries and heather, with views opening ahead over Lower Wensleydale. Go through the gate ahead over the brow and head downhill across the field to exit to the left of a house, onto the road.

Golinglith footbridge

16/7/18 · U·Sunny

13. Ellingstring to Jervaulx Abbey (2.2 miles)

69. Turn right and immediately left down the road into the village of Ellingstring. *(The Penguin Dictionary of British Place Names suggests that 'Ellingstring' comes from the Old English for 'watercourse at the place where eels are caught.')* After 700 yards, turn left at Ruskill Bank Farm into an enclosed lane. Ignore the track that swings to the right in front of a farm building after 50 yards. Pass to the left of this building and continue ahead for 300 yards. Eventually the track bears sharp right and terminates at a metal gate. 20 yards before this gate, leave the track by passing through a wooden gate on the left, into a field.

70. Immediately cross the field half-right to a small gate. Go through the gate and cross the next field diagonally to a hedge. Follow the hedge until you find a gap marked with a square post.

71. Pass through the gap and follow the ancient sunken footway in a north-easterly direction to reach a fence corner. Continue ahead with the fence on the right to reach a ladder stile over a wall.

72. Cross the stile and continue northward with a hedge on your right to exit on a bend in the A6108 road. *Be extremely careful on this dangerous, though short, stretch of main road.*

73. The 'Brymor' tea room and ice cream parlour is up the drive to your left. Lavatories. Walkers welcome.

74. With extreme caution, for the road has no pavement and is very busy, walk ahead, northwards, towards Leyburn. Follow the road for 400 yards to the next road junction where you will see a footpath sign next to the lodge leading into the grounds of Jervaulx Park.

75. Enter the park and go ahead on the track for 100 yards. Just before some trees, where the track swings half right, leave the track and head left across the grass, slowly diverging from the wall of the park. A wooden fence appears ahead of you. Keep to the right of it and make for the ruined Abbey, which can just about be seen through the trees. Join the bridleway that runs through the park. Follow this bridleway keeping the remains of the Abbey on your right. The bridleway crosses a cattle grid, and swings left in front of some old buildings with recent additions. Exit the park onto the A 6108 road.

76. Jervaulx Abbey. Ruins of Cistercian abbey, tea rooms, accommodation. See page 40.
Bus services to Ripon and Leyburn.
Contact: 01677 425203
www.dalesanddistrict.co.uk, and www.dalesbus.org .

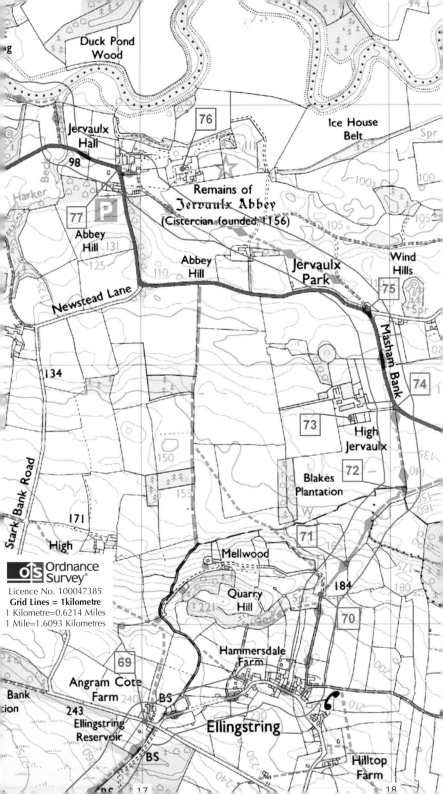

Duck Pond
Wood

Jervaulx
Hall

76

Ice House
Belt

98

Spr

Harker Beck

77

P

Remains of
Jervaulx Abbey
(Cistercian founded 1156)

100

100

Abbey
Hill 131
125

Abbey
Hill

110

Jervaulx
Park

105

105

Wind
Hills

75

Spr

Newstead Lane

Masham Bank

74

134

73

High
Jervaulx

135

150

Blakes
Plantation

72

Stark Bank Road

155

71

160

171

W

150

High

Mellwood

184

180

Quarry
Hill

221

70

Ordnance
Survey®
Licence No. 100047385
Grid Lines = 1kilometre
1 Kilometre=0.6214 Miles
1 Mile=1.6093 Kilometres

Hammersdale
Farm

200

69

Angram Cote
Farm

BS

210

Bank
tion

243
Ellingstring
Reservoir

240

Ellingstring

230

BS

Hilltop
Farm

17

18

14. Jervaulx Abbey to Middleham (4.0 miles)

9 mile

77. Turn right and follow the road for 300 yards. Immediately after crossing Harker Beck, turn right and follow the field track to the River Ure. Turn left and follow the path upstream, with the river on your right, for 1.6 miles, as far as Cover Bridge, passing the confluence of the Ure and Cover.

78. Cross Cover Bridge (public house on left) and follow the road around to the left, re-joining the riverside path just after the public house.

79. Follow the bank of the River Cover upstream, with the river on your left, for half a mile, passing through attractive riverside woodland, and a number of small gates and stiles to a set of stepping stones across the river. Do not cross. The route stays on the north bank of the river.

80. 150 yards after the stepping stones, the riverside path enters a field. At the far end of the field, go through a gate in the right hand corner. Continue on the woodland path for 400 yards, river always on the left, to a second field. 50 yards into the field, cross a broken wall. 200 yards further along the riverside, cross a further wall and turn right. Keeping this wall on your right hand side, ascend across fields toward Middleham. Just after a building, which is to your right, the path goes through a stile/gate and continues with the wall on the left. Over the brow, Middleham Castle appears, straight ahead.

81. As you now descend into Middleham, the path becomes an enclosed lane with the castle on your left. Turn left across the front of the castle to reach the road. The market cross, where the trail finishes, is to your right, down the hill, in the centre of the town.

82. Middleham. 12th century castle, tea rooms, pubs, accommodation, lavatories, buses to Ripon and Leyburn. See page 41

Track alongside Middleham Castle

Market Cross - Middleham

15. Otley

Otley is a medieval town with substantial nineteenth century additions. It owes its existence to the river crossing: a handsome medieval bridge spans the Wharfe. The sturdy parish church, built from the local gritstone, commands Kirkgate, and the strenuous denominational battles of the nineteenth century have left their mark in the form of a number of fine non-conformist churches, and a handsome Roman Catholic church. 150 years ago, these various churches, along with an equally fine profusion of public houses, and the Mechanics' Institute (in Cross Green), served a population that was engaged chiefly in the manufacture of textiles, paper and printing presses. The surrounding farms were served by two cattle markets, one of which survives. Lawbreakers were brought to book at the Courthouse, in Courthouse Street - a building now transformed into a vibrant arts centre and café (otleycourthouse.org.uk). At the centre of the town is the Buttercross Market, punctuated by the Jubilee Clock Tower, and backed by a dramatic view of the Chevin, the hillside that dominates the town. Look above the modern shop fronts and you will see that the buildings that they

deface are commonly Georgian, or even earlier. Pick your way through the ginnels and little cobbled side streets that lead away from the market place and you will find further old buildings. The 21st century leaves its architectural mark too: look for the new public library, in Nelson Street, close to the bus station. The library houses the Tourist Information Centre, which is open 7 days a week (01943 462485). Otley is a Walkers are Welcome Town: see p42. A calendar of events throughout the year in Otley is available at visitotley.co.uk.

Public transport links. From the bus station there are services to Leeds, Ilkley, Skipton, Bradford, Harrogate and Leeds-Bradford airport. A shuttle bus connects Otley with Menston station for trains to Bradford and Leeds, which connect with the national rail mainline network. For further transport information, call MetroLine on 0113 245 7676 or visit the Metro website at wymetro.com. The Six Dales Trail website, sixdalestrail.org.uk, gives details of some of the accommodation available in Otley.

Specialist Shop for walkers.
Chevin Trek, 34 Gay Lane, (Leeds Road) Otley, West Yorkshire, LS21 1BR, 01943 851166. chevintrek.co.uk.

Thomas Chippendale

16. Pateley Bridge

Pateley Bridge is a small market town on the River Nidd. Its Tourist Information Centre is open 7 days a week in the summer months, from 10.00 to 17.00 on weekdays and 10.00 to 13.00 on Sundays (18 High Street, Pateley Bridge, HG3 5AW. 01423 711147). It carries information about the excellent local museum (nidderdalemuseum.com), and accommodation and campsite information. At times when the Pateley Bridge office is closed, contact Harrogate Tourist Information Centre on 01423 537300. Information about both Pateley Bridge and Harrogate can be found at harrogate.gov.uk

Public transport: Service number 24 runs from Pateley Bridge to Harrogate, all year round and is operated by Transdev in Harrogate. (01423 566061). www.harrogatebus.co.uk. Transdev also operate the excellent No 36 service to Ripon and Leeds from Harrogate, which runs every 15 minutes. Buses to Ripon from Pateley Bridge are limited to Sundays and Bank Holidays in the Summer (and one journey on Thursdays, operated by Murgatroyd Travel Services - 01943 880249). Pateley Bridge is also served by other Dales Bus services on Sundays and bank Holidays in the Summer. Check before travelling: dalesbus.org

Specialist Shop for Walkers: Sypeland Outdoor,
15 High Street, Pateley Bridge, HG3 5AP, 01423 712922,

High Street – Pateley Bridge

17. Jervaulx Abbey

Founded in 1156, Jervaulx was a Cistercian abbey, the daughter house of the abbey at Byland. The Cistercian Order was based on the austerity taught by St Benedict. Under the leadership of Bernard of Clairvaux, Cistercian monks set out to establish themselves in wild and inhospitable areas where they could dedicate their lives to prayer, study, meditation and manual labour. The north of England offered just such an environment. Viking settlement during the Anglo-Saxon period had led to the destruction of many of the older monasteries: the Cistercians filled this spiritual vacuum with monastic houses like those at Rievaulx, Fountains, Byland and Jervaulx. Jervaulx was not the first monastic house in the Vale of Ure. An earlier monastery was established at nearby Fors, but the land there was poor and so it was moved to its present site. Although Cistercian monks committed themselves to lives of austerity, paradoxically because of the monks' industriousness, their abbeys grew to be very prosperous, agricultural estates. At the height of Jervaulx's prosperity, the Abbey owned half of the valley and was renowned for breeding horses, a tradition that remains in the area to the present day. It was also the original home of Wensleydale cheese.

Jervaulx was severely ravaged and pillaged during the Dissolution of Monasteries in the mid-sixteenth century. Two centuries later, in common with numbers of ruined abbeys – Fountains, for example – the 18th century fashion for the picturesque and romantic made owners set their ruins as the focal points of carefully-landscaped parkland. The site at Jervaulx was purchased by its present owners in 1971. It remains a place of great beauty and tranquillity, and is famed for having over 180 species of wild flowers growing within its walls.

18. Middleham and its castle

Middleham, a small market town clustered below the castle, is now the base for a number of racehorse stables. Strings of horses can often be seen going to, and returning from, the gallops above the town.

The castle is late 12th century and from it, the mighty Neville family dominated much of northern England. Richard III spent much of his youth at Middleham. After his death, in 1485, at the Battle of Bosworth, the castle and its lands were seized by the new king, Henry VII. The building fell into disrepair, but found a new use during the Civil War of the seventeenth century, when it was used to house prisoners. The castle passed into private hands in 1662, after the end of the Civil War. In 1925, by which time it was in ruins, much of its stone having been carted away for use in other buildings, the castle passed into the care of the Office of Works – later English Heritage. www.middlehamonline.com is a useful source of information and contains links to other websites with more detail. And of course there is always Wikipedia.

The Tourist Information Centre covering Middleham is at nearby Leyburn (Leyburn Tourist Information Centre, The Dales Haven, Market Place, Leyburn DL8 5BJ. Tel: 01969 623814).
The information centre is open all year (seasonal times apply).
For further tourist information, consult www.richmondshire.gov.uk.

Public Transport. Operated by Dales and District Buses (01677 425203 www.dalesanddistrict.co.uk.) Bus service number 159 runs from Middleham to Leyburn approximately every two hours through the daytime. The journey takes five minutes. From Leyburn there are links eastward to Ripon, Richmond and Hawes. Dales Bus Service 820 / 821 runs on Summer Sundays and Bank Holidays between Otley and Richmond via Summerbridge, Pateley Bridge, Ripon, Masham, Middleham and Leyburn, with connections at Otley to Dewsbury and Wakefield. All routes and times for Dales Bus services are for the Summer period only. Winter times and routes may vary or not operate at all. (www.dalesbus.org). For journey planning visit Traveline: metrojourneyplanner and, for travel in the Dales www.wymetro.com. At the head of Wensleydale, at Garsdale railway station, the spectacular Settle to Carlisle line can be boarded. Train services run north to Carlisle and south to Leeds, via Skipton.

19. Walkers are Welcome

'Walkers are Welcome' (WAW) towns and villages across the UK are places that have something special to offer walkers of all ages and abilities, and provide a variety of outstanding walking experiences. The national organisation is a non-profit making 'Community Interest Company', governed by a Steering Committee made up of representatives from WAW communities across the UK. The nationwide initiative was launched in 2007 to encourage towns and villages to be "welcoming to walkers". The network has expanded rapidly and there are now over 120 locations across the UK that have joined this innovative community-led scheme to benefit from WAW accreditation.

Its aims are to encourage and support towns and villages to:

- be attractive destinations for walkers with top quality information on local walks
- offer local people and visitors excellent walking opportunities within their areas
- ensure that footpaths and facilities for walkers are maintained, improved and well-signposted
- raise the profile of local areas as attractive tourist destinations
- promote the health benefits of walking and increase participation
- encourage the use of public transport

You will know you are in a WAW community when you see the familiar black and gold logo in shops, cafes, businesses, B&B's etc..
See www.walkersarewelcome.org.uk for lots of information on each of the accredited communities in the UK.

Otley www.waw-otley.org.uk was awarded accreditation in 2008. Since then, twelve self-guided fully signposted walking routes have been developed and published. These include the Six Dales Trail, and in 2016 the 28-mile 'Welcome Way' that connects Otley with the WAW communities of Burley in Wharfedale, Baildon and Bingley.

Kate Ashbrook, our Patron of Walkers are Welcome and President of the Ramblers, says:
"Walkers Are Welcome has grown at an astonishing pace as more and more towns and villages have seen the benefits of accreditation and have come on board. Now walkers know that, if they see the friendly footprint logo, they are assured of a warm welcome throughout the town, and a good path network and waymarked walks round about. So everyone benefits – visitors, residents and the local economy."

20. The Countryside Code and general information

. Be safe - plan ahead and follow any signs. Even when going out locally, it's best to get the latest information about where and when you can go. For example, your rights to go onto some areas of open land may be restricted while work is carried out, for safety reasons, or during breeding seasons. Follow advice and local signs, and be prepared for the unexpected.

. Leave gates and property as you find them. Please respect the working life of the countryside, as our actions can affect people's livelihoods, our heritage, and the safety and welfare of animals and ourselves.

. Protect plants and animals and take your litter home. We have a responsibility to protect our countryside now and for future generations, so make sure you do not harm animals, birds, plants or trees.

. Keep dogs under close control. The countryside is a great place to exercise dogs, but it's every owner's duty to make sure their dog is not a danger or nuisance to farm animals, wildlife or other people.

. Consider other people. Showing consideration and respect for other people makes the countryside a pleasant environment for everyone, at home, at work and at leisure.

Confluence Ure and Cover

Good general websites for all information:
www.visitharrogate.co.uk
www.yorkshiredales.org.uk

21. The Ramblers' Association

The Ramblers' Association (also known as The Ramblers) is the major walkers' organisation that has, at its heart, the protection of rights of way – the public footpaths and bridleways – upon which all walkers depend. The Ramblers' record of preventing the closure of existing rights of way is second to none. The so-called "Right to Roam Act" (more properly the year 2000 Countryside and Rights of Way Act) for which the Ramblers campaigned for many years, opened up areas of moorland, mountain, heath and downland from which walkers were previously forbidden. In the north of England, it has opened up for walkers mile upon mile of Pennine moorland, for instance, the Bronte Moors, Denton Moor, and Fountains Earth Moor through which The Six Dale Trail passes. As a result of continuing pressure from the Ramblers, the government has renewed its commitment to completing the English Coast Path (which goes along the whole of the English coast) by 2020. Less spectacularly, but just as important, the Ramblers, through an extensive regional and local network, works to keep local footpaths open, signposted and free from obstruction.

Everyone who walks in Britain is indebted to the Ramblers' Association for its ceaseless work to protect and enhance walkers' rights. All walkers are encouraged to join, whether it be just to give material support, or equally to participate actively by taking part in the extensive programme of led -walks o perhaps by becoming involved in footpath work.

The Ramblers' Association, 2nd floor, Camelford House,
87-90 Albert Embankment, London, SE1 7TW.
020 7339 8500.
www.ramblers.org.uk/join

Walkers approaching Roundhill Reservoir